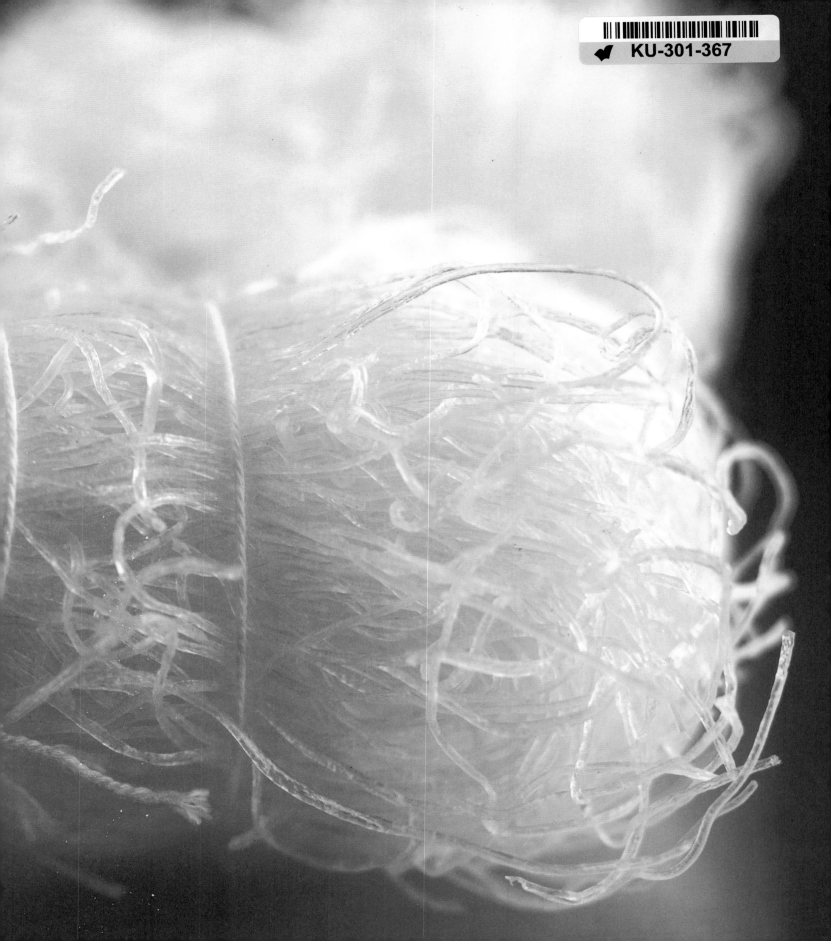

Flavours of

China

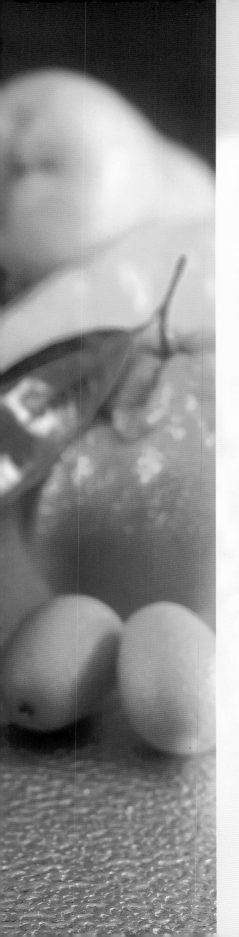

Flavours of
China

Clare Ferguson

photography by **Jeremy Hopley**

RYLAND
PETERS
& SMALL

Designer **Megan Smith**

Design Assistant **Stuart Edwards**

Editor **Elsa Petersen-Schepelern**

Creative Director **Jacqui Small**

Publishing Director **Anne Ryland**

Production **Meryl Silbert**

Food Stylist **Clare Ferguson**

Stylist **Wei Tang**

Photographer's Assistant **Catherine Rowlands**

Indexer **Hilary Bird**

Author Photograph **Graeme Harris**

Dedication
To my husband, Ian Ferguson, for his encouragement.

Acknowledgements
My thanks to Jeremy Hopley, Wei Tang, Catherine Rowlands, Nicky Rogerson,
Karl Rixon, Megan Smith, Elsa Petersen-Schepelern and Fiona Smith –
The A Team. Thanks to Christine Boodle for technical advice, and to Guillaume
de Rougemont for his help with the translations. Thanks also to my suppliers;
butchers David Lidgate and Kingsland, and greengrocers the Michanicou
Brothers and Hyams & Cockerton. My appreciation also to my agents Fiona
Lindsay and Linda Shanks.

Notes
All spoon measurements are level unless otherwise specified.
Ovens should be preheated to the specified temperature. If using a fan
oven, cooking times should be reduced according to the manufacturer's
instructions.

First published in Great Britain in 1998
by Ryland Peters & Small
Cavendish House, 51–55 Mortimer Street, London W1N 7TD

Text © Clare Ferguson 1998
Design and photographs © Ryland Peters & Small 1998

Produced by Toppan, Hong Kong
Printed and bound in China

ISBN 1 900518 62 7

A CIP record for this book is available from the British Library

contents

introduction

China has produced one of the world's greatest cuisines. Though its techniques evolved from the fierce wood or charcoal-burning stoves, modern Chinese cooks have adapted these methods to efficient modern equipment. Their essential philosophy remains however – the use of fresh produce, complex flavours in preserves and pickles, elegant and subtle dried, salted, fermented and cured condiments, superbly flavoured stocks, sauces and dips, and wonderfully textured noodles, breads, dumplings and rice dishes.

Though modern advances in agriculture and technology mean increased harvests of wheat, millet, soya beans and rice, as well as fish, meat and poultry, China has not forgotten its past hardships of crop failures and famine, so nothing is ever wasted.

The celebration of the seasons is important, as are the Buddhist and Taoist principles of yin and yang (female and male). Texture, colour, strength or subtlety of flavour, tastes of salt, sweet or sour – all give Chinese food its special appeal. Match-making of ingredients and combining foods harmoniously is at the heart of Chinese cooking, and they regard food and health part of the same issue.

Chinese cuisine has great virtuosity and falls into four main culinary regions: Peking or Northern, notable for use of lamb, garlic and leeks; Shanghai or Eastern, with sweeter flavours; Szechuan or Western with its spicy, fiery, chilli flavours; and Cantonese or Southern – familiar in the West – where pork and seafood are favourites.

In China, dishes are served all together, as they are prepared, not in courses, the way they are in the West. However, Chinese dishes can be incorporated into the Western style of eating, and many lend themselves to party food. It is in this spirit that the recipes in this book were chosen. Most of the ingredients are available in ordinary supermarkets, while others are easily found in Chinatown shops.

1

2

Chinese ingredients

Many Chinese ingredients, such as soy sauce and noodles, have become so universally popular that we tend to forget their Asian origins. They are very versatile with herbs, vegetables and spices used as much for their therapeutic health qualities as for their flavour.

CHINESE TRINITY

1. The three pivotal flavours in Chinese cooking are colloquially known as the Chinese Trinity. Many dishes begin with these three ingredients, being stir-fried to flavour the cooking oil. They include, from left:

Ginger is usually peeled, then finely sliced, chopped or grated.

Garlic as in other cuisines is peeled, then sliced or crushed. Young bulbs have a milder taste than older ones.

Spring Onions are used cooked in the Trinity, but also chopped or finely sliced in all other cooking methods, and also used raw. They cook instantly in contact with heat, retaining their vivid colour.

CHINESE HERBS AND FLAVOURINGS

2. Of the many fresh herbs and flavourings used in Chinese cooking, the most common available in the West include, from left:

Chillies, originated in Mexico and introduced to Asia by Portuguese traders in the 16th century. Of cayenne type, they are small to medium, with hot clear flavour. Red ones are ripe, green unripe.

Chinese Chives the round-leaf variety is often sold with buds and flowers: the flat-leaf kind has green or yellow leaves. Both have pungent, garlic-like flavour. Ordinary chives may be substituted.

Coriander with its musky, citrus scent, is also known as Chinese parsley and cilantro, used towards the end of cooking, as a garnish.

VEGETABLES

Vegetables occupy pride of place in Chinese cuisine, and many have been adopted into Western cuisines.

3. The bean family includes, clockwise from left:

Mangetout or Snowpeas trim the stem end only, then steam or stir-fry for 1 minute, then use in salads, soups and composite dishes.

Chinese Longbeans are also known as snake beans and yard-long beans. Mild and crunchy, they are chopped and used in stir-fries.

Bean Sprouts are the crisp, pale shoots of the mung bean, prized for their crispness. Though available canned, fresh ones are vastly superior, and they are easy to sprout at home. Chinese cooks pinch off the root ends and nip out the bean from the end of the shoot. Refrigerate in airtight containers to preserve crunch.

4. Gourds, roots and rhizomes include, from rear:

Winter Melon (rear left) is a pale green squash, with a powdery snowy coating on the skin. Succulent with delicate flavour.

Bitter Melon (rear centre) is an acquired taste. Cut in half, remove the inner membrane, then blanch before using.

Silk Squash (rear right) is best eaten young. Trim off the sharp ridges, slice, then stir-fry or braise. Courgette-like in texture.

Aubergine (centre) Chinese and Japanese aubergines are thinner than the common variety, and often shorter. They have a more delicate flavour and need not be salted before use.

Shallots (front left) reddish-violet in colour, sold in in clusters, is the variety used in South-east Asian and sometimes in Chinese cooking.

Lotus Root unpeeled (right front) and peeled and sliced (front centre)

is a rhizome with astringent flavour. Porous and fibrous, it is peeled and sliced crossways into acidulated water before cooking.

5. Other popular Chinese root vegetables include, from left:
White Radish, Daikon or Mooli is large with white skin or smaller with greenish skin. Used hot or cold, and prized for its crisp texture.
Jicama or Yam Bean is a round, tan-coloured root with crisp white flesh. Peeled and sliced, its flavour is similar to water chestnuts.
Taro is a brown tuber with creamy interior. Used in China since prehistoric times in many ways, including flour, puddings and pastes.

LEAF VEGETABLES

6. The cabbage family includes the most popular vegetables in China.
Chinese Cabbage, Napa Cabbage or Chinese Leaves (rear) has crisp texture and sweet, mild taste.
Front, from left: **Chinese Flowering Cabbage or Choy Sum** has a sweet, mustardy flavour, and can be identified by its yellow flowers.
Chinese Mustard Cabbage or Gai Choy has an astringent, clean fresh taste, it is used in stir-fries, pickles and preserves.
Bok Choy or Pak Choi Crisp and succulent, popular in stir-fries. Two varieties of the baby versions shown here with white or green stems.
Chinese Broccoli (Chinese Kale) has white flowers and chard-like taste.

7. Other popular leaves used in Chinese cooking, becoming more widely available include, from left:
Pea Shoots are the tender young green leaves and tendrils of the mangetout or snowpea. Use the day you buy them as a garnish in soups or stir-fries. Becoming popular in Western haute cuisine.
Water Spinach, unrelated to ordinary spinach, cooked the same way.
Chinese Celery has intense, celery flavour in leaves and stems.

CHINESE FRUIT

Fruit is usually eaten raw at any time of day, but especially at the end of a meal. Some fruits are also poached in syrup and other favourite varieties are available canned.

1. Pomelo (rear) huge yellow citrus fruit with scented rind (good for preserves), thick white pith and dense, crunchy segmented interior with flavour similar to grapefruit.
Chinese Pear (centre) is similar to Japanese or nashi pear, distinguished by its pointed top and long black stem. Its elegant apple-crisp white flesh is eaten raw.
Mangosteen (front left) the hard skin is sliced around the equator. Pull off top 'cap'. Inside are sweet, lychee-like juicy segments.
Kumquat (front centre) is a miniature citrus fruit, with tart flesh. Eaten fresh, preserved, pickled, candied or cooked in syrup.
Lychees (front right) have a thin reddish skin, pearly flesh and glossy brown seed. Sold fresh or canned, intensely scented.
Longans (not shown), with flavour similar to lychees, are highly prized. Brown felty skin, sold in bunches like large grapes.

2. Starfruit or Carambola green (left) when unripe, ripening to juicy yellow (second left) with brown ridges, which can be trimmed before eating raw or poached in syrup.
Persimmon (centre) honey-sweet, with orange-red skin and dense, sweet, mellow juicy flesh. Eat raw when very ripe, or poach in syrup. Also known as sharon or kaki fruit
Rose Apple (right) is apple-green, sometimes tinged with rose pink. Subtle sweetness and crunchy apple texture.

3. Guava (from left, three varieties shown; large green, small green, small yellow) intensely scented fruit with flesh ranging from white to yellow or dark pink. All parts are edible. Eaten fresh, or with a sprinkling of salt or chilli; also made into jam or jelly.

Custard Apple (right) soft, heart-shaped fruit with knobbly or 'tiled' skin. Flesh is intensely sweet and creamy buds. Glossy black seeds are inedible.

CANS AND PRESERVES

4. Vegetables used fresh, blanched, canned or preserved include, from left:
Bamboo Shoots blanched (left) and canned (second left), the shoots of winter bamboo, give crisp texture to composite dishes. Sold fresh in Chinese markets, they must be peeled and blanched to remove toxins.
Water Chestnuts available canned (right) or vacuum packed. Also fresh (front) in Chinese markets, to be peeled before use. The white flesh is crisp and crunchy.
Preserved Vegetable (rear) is a savoury, sweet-sour pickle with strong taste and smell, used as a condiment. Vegetables may be mustard greens, turnip or cabbage.

CHINESE MUSHROOMS

5. Fresh and dried mushrooms are used alone and in combination for flavour and texture. Clockwise from left are:
Oyster Mushrooms shown here are yellow, pink and grey. Subtle flavour, always used fresh. Said to taste of the sea, though the name refers to the colour of the grey variety.
Shiitake Mushrooms are available fresh (right) and dried (centre). Tough stems are always discarded, the caps often sliced before cooking. Dried shiitakes are reconstituted in boiling water; the water is then discarded.
Chinese Straw Mushrooms (front right) are sold canned. They have a smooth and meaty texture and attractive appearance, thanks to the silky, shiny black-fleshed cap.
Black Fungus, Cloud Ears or Wood Ears (front centre) are usually dried, reconstituted in hot water, chopped and added to composite dishes. They have subtle, mild flavour, and are prized for colour and gelatinous texture.

1

4

2

3

5

CHINESE SAUCES

Chinese oils, sauces and pastes are used in various quantities as dips, flavourings, cooking mediums or seasonings. They include:

1. Yellow Bean Sauce (left) – a purée of fermented yellow soya beans, crushed and mixed with flour, salt and water. Sold in cans or jars.
Salted Black Beans (rear) **and Black Bean Sauce** (right) fermented soya beans with intense, savoury saltiness. Use the beans dry or mashed into pastes or sauces. Sauce is sold in jars or cans.

2. Hoisin Sauce (rear) is made from soya beans, salt, flour, sugar, vinegar, garlic, sesame oil and chilli. Thick, fruity, tangy, salty and sweet, used in red-cooking and as a condiment, sauce and dip.
Plum Sauce (front) is made from plums, ginger, chilli, spices, vinegar and sugar. Stores well in the refrigerator for some weeks.

3. Oyster Sauce (left) is a thick, salty, slightly sweet Cantonese-style sauce made from oysters and soy sauce. Refrigerate when opened.
Chinese Shrimp Sauce or Paste (right) – thick, pungent, salty purée of fermented shrimp. Very different from South-east Asian versions.

4. Soy Sauce is made from fermented, salted soya beans. Superior (more expensive) quality is very pure and production is slower. Dark (thick) soy is richer and less salty. Light (thin) soy is paler, saltier and discolours food less. Used as condiment, dip, sauce or flavouring.
From left: **Dark Superior Soy Sauce, Light Superior Soy Sauce** and **Mushroom Soy Sauce** (which is infused with dried straw mushrooms). Not shown is **Shrimp Soy Sauce** (infused with dried shrimp).

5. Introduced by Portuguese traders in the 16th century, chilli has become a favourite Chinese ingredient, especially in Szechuan.
Chilli Sauce (rear) is a mixture of crushed fresh chillies, vinegar, salt and plums. Available extra hot, hot or sweet, which is milder. Used as a condiment, dip or sauce, it is usually sold in bottles or cans.
Chilli Oil (front) is made from chillies infused in oil. Sold in bottles as a condiment or sauce, with fiery taste.

RICE WINE AND RICE VINEGAR (not shown)

Rice Vinegars Red vinegar is slightly sweet and salty, used as a dipping sauce. Black vinegar is rich but mild, similar to balsamic. Used with noodles and in sauces. Sweet vinegar is dark and thick, flavoured with sugar and star anise, used in braised pork dishes. White vinegar is clear and mild, used in sweet and sour dishes.
Chinese Rice Wine or Shaohsing is used for drinking (usually warmed) and cooking. If unavailable, dry sherry may be substituted.

CHINESE SPICES

6. The spices and flavourings that give Chinese food its distinctive taste and aroma include, from rear:

Five-spice Powder (rear left) is an aromatic mixture of star anise, cinnamon, cloves, Szechuan peppercorns and liquorice root. Store in airtight glass in a dark place.

Candy Crystal Sugar (rear right) s cane sugar in large crystal form, sold in lumps and fragments. Pure clean taste, keeps indefinitely. White or soft brown sugar may be substituted.

Cassia Bark (centre right) is taken from a type of cassia or laurel tree, darkish red-brown and flattish. More scented than paler curled quills of **Cinnamon Bark** (centre left) from a different kind of laurel.

Dried Tangerine Peel (front left) is often combined with star anise and Szechuan pepper. Do not substitute candied peel. It is easy to air-dry, oven-dry or microwave-dry your own peel – tangerine, orange or other citrus. Thread onto strings and store.

Star Anise (centre front) is an 8-pointed star-shaped pod with anise-flavoured seeds. Used whole in Chinese cooking, but removed before eating. Also available in powder form, and as a component of 5-spice.

Szechuan Peppercorns (front right) are small, reddish peppercorns with a distinct woodsy aroma and slightly numbing effect on the tongue. Especially aromatic when lightly toasted.

COOKING OILS

7. Chinese cooks prefer oils with a high smoke point and little flavour of their own, so the flavour of the food shines through. From left:

Peanut Oil: is also known as arachide or groundnut oil.

Corn Oil (right) is polyunsaturated is good for stir-frying and very good for deep-frying, reasonable for stir-frying

Soy bean oil (not shown) is healthy, neutral. Good mix with other oils.

SESAME INGREDIENTS

8. A favourite Chinese ingredient that appears in many forms. Clockwise from left are:

White and Black Sesame Seeds have a sweet, nutty taste and are often toasted at home before use. High in oil-content, they can become rancid and musty in taste. Store in an airtight container and discard if rancid smells develop.

Sesame Oil is a thick aromatic oil, made from roasted sesame seeds, and sold in bottles. Use as a condiment or to give foods sheen. Expensive and highly-scented, it is rarely used in frying, but if so, it should be combine with another oil with a high smoke-point.

Sesame Seed Paste is also known as sesame paste or sesame butter. It is used in sauces and as a flavour and texture ingredient in dishes. Darker than Middle Eastern tahini paste.

NOODLES

1. Bean and rice noodles, clockwise from left:
Bean thread or cellophane noodles are made
from mung bean flour. Put in a bowl, cover
with boiling water, drain, then serve or reheat.
Dried flat rice noodles, stir-fry rice noodles
and rice sticks are made from rice flour,
ranging from thin vermicelli 1.5 cm rice
sticks. Packet cooking instructions are
rarely accurate. Soak in boiling water for
1–2 minutes or hot water for 6–12 minutes
depending on thickness. Drain and serve
or reheat. Use steamed, poached, stir-fried,
deep-fried or in composite dishes.
Fresh noodles are rinsed but not soaked.

2. Egg noodles, made from wheat flour and
enriched with egg include, from rear:

Fresh egg noodles coated in oil as a
preservative. Rinse, then cook briefly.
Dried egg noodles should be boiled in salted
water. Times vary: follow packet directions.
Fresh egg noodles should be rinsed then
cooked for 3–4 minutes in oil or liquid.

3. Wheat noodles are cooked in boiling salted
water, then drained and served. From rear:
White wheat noodles are cooked 4–6 minutes
or according to packet instructions.
Wheat vermicelli noodles and **Yellow dried**
wheat noodles are cooked 3–5 minutes or
according to packet instructions.
Fresh wheat noodles (right) and **Shanghai**
noodles (left) should be rinsed briefly in
boiling water. Drain and cook 3–4 minutes
or to taste. Drain and serve.

RICE

4. *Fan*, **the Chinese word for rice, also means**
simply 'food', reflecting the importance of
rice in Chinese culture. Clockwise from left:
Fragrant Thai rice though associated with
South-east Asian cooking, is highly prized
in China for its scent.
Long grain rice though not traditional
in China, is now widely used there and in
Chinese restaurants around the world. The
grains are fluffy and separate when cooked.
Glutinous rice is more often identified with
Japanese cooking, but is used in China
mostly for sweet dishes, because of its
sticky qualities.
Rice flour gives a fine crumbly quality to
baked goods, and was formerly used instead
of cornstarch as a thickening agent.

BEAN CURD AND WHEAT GLUTEN

5. **Protein-rich products used in vegetarian dishes, clockwise from left:**

Wheat gluten or *seitan* bland in taste, but absorbs flavours of other ingredients. Sold in powder form, or fresh, as shown here.

Bean curd or *tofu* in various forms; fried and canned (left), **freshly fried** (right), **preserved** (far right) **and fresh** (front) are high in protein, but bland in taste. All forms absorb the flavours of other ingredients.

CHINESE WRAPPERS

6. Clockwise from top left;

Dumpling wrappers of wheat flour, for dim sum.

Spring roll wrappers are transparent paper-like sheets made of rice flour, sold fresh or frozen, in squares or rounds.

Wonton skins Silky, pale yellow, 7.5 or 10 cm wide squares, made from wheat flour, egg and water. Fresh or frozen: if frozen, thaw slowly or they stick. Wrap until ready for use.

Pancakes (also known as mushu wrappers or Mandarin pancakes) 23-cm discs of wheat flour dough. Used as wrappers for Peking Duck or Mu Shu Pork.

2

3

4

5

6

Chinese cooking techniques

Chinese stir-frying and steaming have been adopted by many other cuisines. Cleaver-chopping, however, has been largely supplanted by the food processor, but produces excellent texture in minced meats and chopped herbs.

Wok stir-frying

Woks are usually 30–34 cm in diameter, with 2 loop handles or one long wooden handle. Traditional woks have a rounded base, and best used on a gas cooktop rather than electric. Accessories include a lid and a metal rack, which is clipped onto the edge of the wok to drain or reserve food during the stir-frying process. Also useful is the wooden-handled, metal, shovel-like wok spoon (**1**), or a long-handled wooden spoon. Before first use, iron woks must be cleaned, heated with oil, then wiped and dried well. Lightly oil again between uses.

To stir-fry, heat the wok, add the oil and heat until very hot, swirling the oil around to coat the surface. Add the aromatics, then the other ingredients, one variety at a time, and cook, tossing and stirring, until they are set or coated and the juices are sealed in. As each is ready, transfer to the rack or a plate and continue until all are done. Return all to the wok, add the liquid specified in the recipe, 'steam-stir' (**2**) until cooked, then serve immediately.

Steaming

Bamboo steamers of various sizes are sold in oriental supermarkets, and are attractive enough to use also as serving dishes.

Buy one or more tiers (they have perforated bases to let in the steam), plus a lid to fit that size. Metal 2- and 3-tier steamers are also sold in Asian stores.

Put the food into the steamer base, set the base over a wok, saucepan or frying-pan containing boiling liquid (for steam) and cover with the lid. Some foods sit directly in the steamer base, others, such as fish, are set on a heatproof plate, and still others, such as the Lion Head Meatballs (page 50) on greaseproof paper. Always leave gaps so the steam can penetrate.

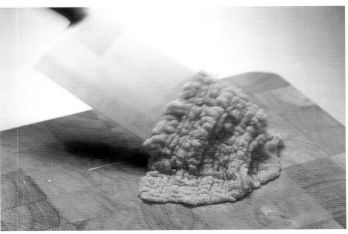

Using Chinese Cleavers

Chinese cleavers are sold in Chinese and other cookware stores. Many cooks prefer the consistency produced by cleavers, rather than by a mincer, which squeezes rather than cuts the meat. From above:

Best-quality cleavers are made of tempered carbon steel and have either metal or wooden handles.

Chopping with cleavers Chinese cooks chop foods using two sharp cleavers, giving a result similar to machine-grinding or chopping in a food processor, especially for meat, fish and chicken. Lift and drop each cleaver quickly in succession, letting the weight of the cleavers do the hard work.

Flipping with cleavers To achieve an even consistency, periodically flip the meat with the flat of the cleaver and chop the other side.

Zhu Fan

Chinese Boiled Rice

In Chinese, *fan* is the word for 'cooked rice' and for 'meal' and in many parts of the country, particularly the south, every meal contains rice. Rice cooking is taken to a high art, and its selection, treatment and serving methods are regarded as of great importance.

Most cooks prefer long grain rice, and the basic recipe for cooking this kind of rice is given below. Other cooks prefer other kinds of rice, including fragrant Thai-style rice for special occasions, and medium and short grain types for savoury use. Sweet, sticky or glutinous rice is used for puddings, celebrations and sweet doughs (cooking methods are given on page 19). Experiment and discover which types of rice you prefer for each dish – but well-cooked classic plain white rice has wonderful fragrance.

In China, rice is cooked in minimal amounts of water, though it is often washed or soaked in water first. The best way to measure is by volume. In China the general rule is 1 cup of raw rice to 1¼–1½ cups of boiling water – the usual Western method is to cook 1 cup of raw rice to 2 cups of boiling water.

1 cup long grain white rice
1¼ cups boiling water

Makes 3 cups

Wash the rice carefully in a sieve until the water runs clear. Drain well. Pour the boiling water into a heavy-based saucepan with a tight lid. Add the rice, stir and return to the boil over high heat. Turn the heat to low, stir once, then cook, uncovered, for 5 minutes.

Cover and simmer on the lowest possible heat for 15 minutes. Do not lift the lid. Remove the pan from the heat or turn off the heat. Let stand, undisturbed, for 10 minutes more. All the water will be absorbed, and little holes will show on top. Lift the lid and gently fluff up the rice with a fork. This method is the same for short and long grain white rice: only the water volume is a little different.

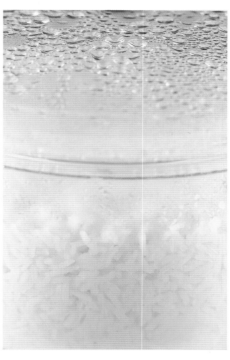

OTHER RICE VARIETIES:

Thai Jasmine Rice or Fragrant Rice
Thai and other South-east Asian perfumed
rice are slightly glutinous or sticky. Note that
glutinous rice does not contain gluten.

1 cup Thai jasmine rice or fragrant rice
½ cup boiling water
Soak the rice in cold water to cover for
1 hour. Drain and transfer to a saucepan,
add the boiling water and cook for
15 minutes. Let stand 10 minutes before
serving. Alternatively, cook on a layer
of muslin in a steamer.

Medium or Short Grain White Rice

1 cup medium or short grain white rice,
**   well washed in cold water**
1 cup boiling water
Wash the rice well in cold water, then cook
as in the main recipe. Let stand 10 minutes
before serving.

Black Sweet Rice

1 cup black sweet rice
1 cup boiling water
Wash the rice well in cold water. Drain
and transfer to a saucepan, add the boiling
water and cook for 25 minutes. Let stand
10 minutes before serving. Alternatively,
cook on a layer of muslin in a steamer.

Note: Electric Rice Cookers

In modern Chinese kitchens, the electric
rice cooker has become an essential
tool, especially for those who cook for large
families. It is the easiest way to cook perfect
rice – no matter which variety – with
minimal attention. Its other great advantage
is that it keeps the rice warm or hot until the
rest of the meal is ready.

If using an electric rice cooker, follow
the cooking instructions given with the
appliance, especially if you want to keep
the rice hot over a longish period.

The soups of China are many and various. Shark's fin and bird's nest soups are two of the most famous examples – mainly, these days, confined to epicurean banquets or grand state events, because the ingredients are rare and exclusive. But on a daily basis nourishing soups of all kinds are created and served all over China. Soup does not come at the start of a meal as in the West: it is more likely to come later on, though, strictly, all the dishes are put on the table at once for family meals.

Dim sum, the small meals or little dishes served between meals, are popular in China. Popularly called *tien-hsin* or *tim-sam*, their name means something to 'dot the heart' or 'touch your heart', and many delicious foods come into this category.

tang, dian xin

soups and little dishes

Lunchtime meals may include a selection of dim sum with several dipping sauces – a pleasant, light way to eat. Early morning snacks and late night nibbles may also include dim sum, and in Chinese restaurants all over the world, push-carts full of tiered bamboo steamers, fully loaded with dozens of variations, are wheeled past tables of avid customers.

These are versatile recipes: use them grouped as a light meal, with drinks, served as first courses at dinner – or just eat them by themselves with Chinese tea, for pleasure!

Shao mai (pronounced 'shoe-my', meaning 'cook and sell') are a favourite Cantonese street food. Cooked in layers in a bamboo steamer, they are often one of the dishes served for yum cha, and also make great food for parties. Square wonton skins are cut into rounds either freehand or using a biscuit cutter, then the edges are gathered to form a purse, leaving the top open to show the delicious filling. Serve with your favourite dipping sauce.

Shao Mai

Steamed Dumpling Purses

500 g chicken breast, diced then
  minced
1 teaspoon freshly ground white
  pepper
2 tablespoons vodka or gin
1 medium egg white
3 slices smoked streaky bacon,
  50 g minced fresh pork fat,
  or 4 tablespoons cream
2 teaspoons sesame oil
2 teaspoons grated fresh ginger
2 teaspoons sea salt flakes
2 teaspoons crushed garlic
2 tablespoons finely chopped parsley
4 spring onions, green and white,
  finely chopped
4 water chestnuts, canned or fresh
  and peeled, finely diced
30–45 square wonton skins
sprigs of Chinese chives, chives or
  coriander, to serve

Makes 30–45, Serves 4–6

Mix the chicken, pepper and vodka or gin in a bowl, cover and set aside while the other ingredients are prepared.

In a second bowl whisk the egg white to a froth, then beat in the bacon, pork fat or cream, then the sesame oil, ginger, salt, garlic and parsley.

Slowly beat in the chicken mixture, spring onions and water chestnuts until evenly combined, but do not over-mix. Alternatively, knead it gently together using your hands (the authentic method).

Using a large biscuit cutter, cut a round as large as possible from each square wonton skin. Put 1 tablespoon filling on each wonton skin and, using a small spatula, smooth the mixture almost to the edges.

Put the filled wonton in the palm of one hand and cup your fingers around it, pushing the mixture down with the spatula – you will achieve an open, pleated purse shape. Drop it gently onto a floured clean surface to flatten the bottom and settle the filling.

Arrange the dumplings, without letting them touch each other, on the base of a bamboo steamer or steamers. Heat a wok or pan of boiling water on top of the stove, set the steamer on top and steam, covered, for about 7–10 minutes, refilling the base with boiling water as necessary. Serve hot, topped with Chinese chives, accompanied by your choice of sauces or dips.

During the thirteenth century, when China suffered under repressive Mongol rule, baked Moon Cakes were used to conceal secret messages to be sent between households. These days they are eaten, plot-free, for pleasure. This version is steamed rather than baked, and the airy pastry conceals a filling of sweet pork and black beans, not secret messages!

Rou Bao |

Steamed Pork Buns

Mix the pork and soy sauce in a shallow bowl and stir well. Put the bowl into a steamer and steam until cooked through. Cool, then stir in the bean paste.

Sift the flour, baking powder and sugar together into a bowl. Cut or rub in the lard until crumb-like in texture. Mix 125 ml hand-hot water, vinegar and salt in a bowl, then pour into the flour mixture all at once. Mix to a soft dough, roll into a ball, cover and set aside for 30 minutes.

Cut 8 pieces of baking parchment 10 cm in diameter. Divide the dough into 8, put one piece onto each paper circle, then roll them out into discs about 9 cm in diameter.

Divide the meat mixture into 8 and put one portion in the centre of each disc of dough. Pull up the paper to form a ball. Pinch closed and twist the edges to seal. Remove the paper, brush the bun with sesame oil and put, seam side down, on the same piece of paper. Steam the pork balls in a bamboo steamer set over a wok of boiling water for 20–25 minutes until soft, risen and thoroughly hot.

Note: To keep droplets of condensation from falling onto the buns, put a thin cloth such as muslin across each tier before putting the lid on top.

100 g pork fillet, minced

1 tablespoon dark soy sauce

50 g canned sweet bean paste

315 g plain flour, plus extra for dusting

4 teaspoons baking powder, or

    2 tablespoons if double-acting

3 tablespoons caster sugar

2 tablespoons softened lard or white

    vegetable shortening

½ teaspoon white vinegar

½ teaspoon salt

sesame oil, for brushing

Makes 8, Serves 4

Spring rolls should be lean, crisp and refreshing – the embodiment of spring. Like many Chinese *dim sum* or *yum cha* foods, they make wonderful party snacks. Serve them with your choice of dipping sauce – I like grated ginger in a little sweetened rice vinegar. Keep the spring roll skins covered with plastic so they don't dry out.

Xiao Chun Juan

Miniature Spring Rolls

125 g fresh beansprouts

75 g spring onions, finely sliced

75 g carrots, finely sliced

75 g bamboo shoots, fresh or soaked, finely sliced

75 g fresh shiitake mushrooms, stems discarded, caps finely sliced

5 cm fresh ginger, finely sliced

3 tablespoons peanut oil, plus extra, for frying

50 g bean curd, finely diced

2 teaspoons caster sugar

1 tablespoon light soy sauce

1 tablespoon Chinese rice wine or dry sherry

20 spring roll wrappers or wonton skins

2 tablespoons flour

2 tablespoons water

Makes 36–40, Serves 6–8

Blanch the beansprouts for 1 minute in boiling water, then refresh in iced water. Top and tail them, discarding the ends. Combine these with the other vegetables and the ginger. Heat 3 tablespoons of the oil, add the vegetables and stir-fry for 1–1½ minutes. Add the bean curd, sugar, soy sauce and rice wine and cook for 1 minute longer. Cool. Divide into 8 portions, each will be enough for 4–5 spring rolls.

Cut each wrapper in half diagonally. Put 1 portion of filling on the long side, a third of the way from the edge. Fold the long side over the filling, then fold over the side flaps. Roll up. Mix the flour and water and dab a little of the mixture on the pointed end of the roll. Press to seal. Set the rolls on a lightly floured surface, not touching, until all are made.

Heat the oil to 190°C (375°F) or a little hotter, but do not let it smoke. Deep-fry the rolls 8–10 at a time for 3–4 minutes. Remove using a wire strainer, drain on crumpled kitchen paper and keep hot in a low oven. Let the oil reheat before cooking the next batch.

When all the spring rolls are cooked, serve with your choice of dips, such as chilli sauce, soy sauce, or grated ginger mixed with equal quantities of rice vinegar, sesame oil and runny honey.

Chinese dumpling wrappers are either round or square, and about 7.5–10 cm in diameter (page 14). The round ones, with more body than the square ones, are originally from Northern China and used to make pork or veal dumplings. Square wrappers, also known as wonton skins, are usually identified with Cantonese cooking. They are thinner, softer and include egg as well as flour and water – so they really do stick to the pot and become nicely browned underneath.

Guo Tier |

Pot-sticker Dumplings

250 g pork rump

2 tablespoons dark soy sauce

2 tablespoons pork or veal stock

8 spring onions, finely chopped

2 teaspoons sesame oil

150 g spring cabbage, Savoy cabbage or
   Swiss chard, finely chopped

5 cm fresh ginger, grated

36–45 round dumpling wrappers (*gyoza*),
   about 275 g

4 tablespoons peanut oil, for cooking

pea shoots or watercress sprigs,
   to serve (optional)

Soy-ginger Dipping Sauce:

4 tablespoons light soy sauce

4 tablespoons Chinese black vinegar

2 tablespoons Chinese rice wine or
   dry sherry

1 cm fresh ginger, finely sliced

Makes 36–45, Serves 6–8

Chop the pork to a fine purée using cleavers (page 17) or a food processor – do not buy ready-minced meat. Mix the soy sauce and stock together. Using a wooden spoon, stir the soy-stock mixture into the pork, followed by the spring onions, oil, cabbage and ginger. Alternatively, if using a food processor, add the ingredients one by one, in brief bursts.

Put 1 dumpling wrapper on a board and put 1 neat tablespoon of filling in the centre. Wet the edges of the wrapper and fold them together to make a half moon shape. Pinch the centre of the curve closed and make two pleats on each side. Press to seal, standing the dumpling on its base as you do it. Tap down. Repeat until all the dumplings are made, placing them, without touching, on a baking sheet lined with non-stick paper.

Brush 2 flat-bottomed woks or large frying-pans with the oil. Add the dumplings in a single layer with the frills upward. Fry for 1–2 minutes, then add enough cold water (about 125 ml) to each wok or pan to part-cover. Cover with lids or foil. Cook gently for 10 minutes or until brown underneath, and tender and pale on top, adding a little extra water as the liquid boils away. Transfer to a serving plate.

To make the dipping sauce, mix all the ingredients together, divide between individual bowls, and serve with the dumplings and a few pea shoots, if using.

Note: The pot-stickers can be frozen, uncooked, then cooked from frozen.

Prawn toasts are one of the most popular items served in Chinese *dim sum* teahouses, and are familiar fare in Chinese restaurants around the world. Usually they are made on plain white sliced bread, but thinly sliced French bread is an easy variation. We have used an easy sprinkle of sliced beans and spring onions, but you could also top them with spectacular butterfly-cut prawns.

Xia Duo Si

Prawn Toasts

Spread the slices of bread on trays or a work surface and leave them to air-dry while you prepare the topping.

Using a food processor, chop the prawns to a purée. Add the ginger, lard or bacon and salt and blend, in short bursts, to a smooth purée. Drizzle in the wine, stock and cornflour and purée in short bursts until creamy. Transfer to a bowl and stir in the water chestnuts.

Whisk the egg white in a separate bowl, then fold evenly into the mixture. Using a broad spatula, spread the mixture firmly over the slices of bread.

If using the whole prawns, remove the shells, but leave the tail fins attached. Slit the prawns lengthways leaving them joined at the tail, forming butterfly shapes. Press them, tails curving up, onto the top of the bread. Scatter the remaining slices with sesame seeds, sliced green beans or garlic chives.

Fill a deep saucepan one-third full of oil and heat to 180–190°C (350–375°F). Add several prawn toasts at once, purée-side down, then cook 3–4 minutes or until they rise to the top. Using tongs, turn them over and briefly brown the under surface. Lift out with a slotted spoon and drain on crumpled kitchen paper. Keep them hot in a low oven while you cook remainder. Slice into halves, if preferred. Serve hot.

Only one rule is absolutely paramount when cooking fish and seafood in China – it must be superbly fresh and simply cooked. If you live in an area with a flourishing Chinese community, you will be able to take advantage of the very fresh ingredients on offer – fish, crustacea and shellfish, with shells and scales still shiny and glistening blue, silver or bright red – wonderful

yu, hai xian

fish and seafood

ingredients, piled high in deep, clean ice, sparkling with freshness. It's always worthwhile shopping there, even if you don't plan to cook in the Oriental style.

These days, however, even supermarkets sell good fresh fish and well-kept frozen seafood. Some raw ingredients are probably better snap-frozen – squid and other cephalopods, for instance, have texture that is actually improved by freezing.

Before the invention of commercial freezing, however, the Chinese had made an art out of drying, salting, curing and pickling many kinds of fish and fish products, which were then used to emphasize other flavours or as easy-to-store products for out-of-season eating.

Since fish and seafood are considered a greater delicacy than meat or poultry in China, much emphasis is placed on simple but elegant cooking methods; steaming, stir-frying, tea-smoking and sweet-and-sour treatments for example, enhance taste and appearance.

The classical Chinese smoking technique is to cook the food first then smoke it briefly over high heat. This recipe is the reverse. The food is smoked first over a mixture of flour, sugar, rice, tea leaves and star anise. The result is a combination of smoking, baking, flavouring and steaming. The fish can be either pan-fried immediately, or sealed and refrigerated safely for up to five days before frying. This is a good cooking method for many oily fish – it has the advantage of cooking the food and adding flavour, as well as acting as a short-term preservative.

Cha Xun Gui Rou

Tea-smoked Salmon

4 salmon fillets, 150 g each, or trout, tuna or swordfish

1 tablespoon peanut oil

2 teaspoons grated fresh ginger

2 teaspoons vodka, gin or white rum

2 teaspoons Szechuan peppercorns, roasted and ground

1 teaspoon sea salt flakes, ground

1 tablespoon chilli oil or sesame oil, to serve

Smoking Mixture:

½ **cup plain flour**

½ **cup sugar**

½ **cup rice**

½ **cup jasmine tea**

½ **cup whole star anise**

Serves 4

Cut 3 deep, diagonal slashes through the skin of each salmon fillet. Pat dry on kitchen paper. Mix the oil, ginger, vodka, peppercorns and salt in a bowl and rub or brush well into the fish. Set aside to marinate for about 30 minutes.

Line a wok or roasting tin with heavy-duty foil. Leave extra hanging out at the edges. Add the smoking mixture, stirred together. Set a rack about 7.5 cm above the mixture. Drain the fish and set each fillet on the rack, skin side up. Cover the wok or tin with more heavy-duty foil, loosely pleating it to allow the smoke to circulate. Crimp the top and bottom layers securely together. If a lid is available, set it in place.

Put the wok or tin on top of a gas burner and turn the heat to the highest possible (if using an electric element, pre-heat first until red-hot). Heat until you can smell the smoke, then leave the wok on the heat for 8–10 minutes for gas and 10–15 minutes for electric.

Remove the wok or tin from the stove and let cool, preferably outdoors. Open the foil.

Tip the remaining marinade into a saucepan and cook for about 1 minute. Stir in the chilli oil, then spoon this over the fish, flesh side up. Use immediately or refrigerate in a sealed container for up to 5 days.

When ready to cook the salmon, pre-heat a cast-iron stove-top grill pan or non-stick frying pan brushed with a little oil. When hot, sear the fish for 2 minutes on each side. Serve with rice or noodles, with lightly pickled vegetables or, like Peking Duck (page 44), with a pile of pancakes, hoisin and crisp vegetables.

Any firm white fish such as cod, mullet, haddock or sole will suit this recipe – avoid soft-fleshed fish, which may fall apart. Although the tomato passato and mild paprika are fairly recent, Westernized additions, the sweet-and-sour treatment for fish has been popular for centuries. The fish marinade is what gives such a distinctive Chinese style to this recipe.

Zhu Xun Tang Cu Yu

Sweet and Sour Fish with Bamboo Shoots

Cut the fish diagonally into 5 cm strips. Peel the ginger and slice it finely, and cut the bamboo shoots into 2.5 cm slices.

Mix the sherry, egg white and 2 tablespoons of the cornflour in a shallow dish, add the fish and marinate for about 30 minutes.

Heat the oil in a wok or frying pan, add the fish and stir-fry it quickly until firm, glossy and aromatic, about 2 minutes. Drain the fish and set aside.

Pour off all but 1 tablespoon of oil from the wok or pan, add the garlic, spring onions, ginger, bamboo shoots and green pepper and stir-fry until hot, crisp and aromatic. Stir in the tomato passato, salt and sugar. Mix the stock, sesame oil and the remaining cornflour in a small bowl, then stir into the other ingredients until glossy and thick.

Return the fish to the pan, reheat briefly and serve with rice or noodles.

Note: About 1 teaspoon mild paprika can be added at the same time as the tomato passato to produce a more lively flavour and colour.

500 g white fish fillets, skinned
2.5 cm fresh ginger
125 g bamboo shoots
2 tablespoons dry sherry
1 egg white, lightly beaten
3 tablespoons cornflour
8 tablespoons peanut oil
2 garlic cloves, sliced
4 spring onions, sliced
1 green pepper, deseeded and sliced
4 tablespoons tomato passato or juice
1 teaspoon salt
1 teaspoon sugar
4 tablespoons fish or chicken stock
2 teaspoons dark sesame oil

Serves 4

Traditionally, the last course of a Chinese banquet will include a whole fish, and this recipe is perfect for that purpose – it tastes superb and looks beautiful. When serving the fish, lift off the top fillets first, then remove and discard the backbone before serving the rest of the fillets – the Chinese regard it as very bad luck to turn the fish over. In a restaurant, the waiter often does this for you – and will reassemble the fish after removing the bones. Utter freshness is essential for this recipe, so choose your fish carefully.

Qing Zhu Yu

Steamed Bass with Leeks and Ginger

2 medium sea bass or grey mullet, well
   cleaned (about 750 g)

1 teaspoon salt

2 teaspoons sesame oil

4 spring onions

1 small leek

7.5 cm fresh ginger

2 tablespoons light soy sauce

2 tablespoons Chinese rice wine or sherry

2 tablespoons peanut oil

Serves 4

Pat the fish dry, inside and out, with kitchen paper. Make 5–6 diagonal slashes right to the bone on both sides of the fish. Rub salt and sesame oil into the slashes and around the cavity. Set the fish on a heatproof dish which will fit neatly into the steamer basket, but still allow the steam to circulate.

Cut the spring onions in half crossways, then finely slice them lengthways. Cut the leek into similarly sized pieces. Peel the ginger and cut it into fine matchstick julienne strips. Scatter the leek, ginger and half the spring onions over the fish, pushing some inside the cavity.

Put the fish into a steamer set over a wok or pan of boiling water, cover and cook at high heat for 16–20 minute. Do not allow to boil dry – top up with more boiling water if necessary. Remove the fish. Mix the soy sauce and rice wine together and pour over the fish. Sprinkle with the reserved spring onions and serve.

Delicate, quick and a riot of textures, colours and interesting flavours, this recipe can be used as one of the dishes for a celebration meal with boiled rice or noodles or as part of an easy lunch or supper. Semi-crisp leaves are the finishing touch, but if you prefer they can be briefly stir-fried or steamed.

Chao Gan Bei |

Stir-fried Scallops *with Mangetout and Mushrooms*

15 g dried black fungus (Chinese mushrooms), such as cloud ears

1 tablespoon cornflour

6 tablespoons fish stock or water

2 tablespoons peanut oil

2 garlic cloves, finely sliced into strips

2.5 cm fresh ginger, finely sliced into matchstick strips

350 g prepared scallops, patted dry

4 spring onions, finely sliced diagonally

125 g mangetout

2 teaspoons light soy sauce

a pinch of sugar, to taste

a pinch of salt, to taste

crisp lettuce leaves, such as cos, little gem or webbs, to serve (optional)

Serves 4

Pour boiling water over the mushrooms, let soak for 15–25 minutes, then trim off and discard any tough centre pieces. Drain.

Mix the cornflour and fish stock or water in a small bowl and set aside.

Heat the oil in wok or deep frying-pan. Add the ginger and garlic and stir-fry for 1 minute. Add the scallops, stir-fry for 1 minute, then add the drained mushrooms, spring onions and mangetout, and stir-fry for 1 minute more. Push the stir-fried ingredients to the side of the wok, add the cornflour-stock mixture, and soy sauce, salt and sugar to taste. Stir until thickened, then mix all the pan contents back into this glaze. Reheat briefly and serve on a bed of crisp leaves, if using.

La Jiao Chao Ming Xia

Stir-fried Chilli Prawns

This is one of the old Chinese favourites – plump rosy prawns, squeaky-fresh and minimally cooked in a flavourful, chilli-enhanced glossy sauce. Crispy noodles are an appropriate accompaniment as shown here, but plain boiled rice is also good.

250 g dried instant egg noodles

450 g uncooked king prawns

4 tablespoons peanut oil

1 red pepper, deseeded and diced

1 yellow pepper, deseeded and diced

2 garlic cloves, finely sliced

1 red chilli, deseeded and sliced (optional)

2.5 cm fresh ginger, sliced

1 tablespoon sugar

1 tablespoon rice wine or dry sherry

2 tablespoons sweet chilli sauce

1 tablespoon light soy sauce

1 teaspoon cornflour

4 spring onions (optional)

Serves 4

Put the noodles into a bowl, cover with boiling water and set aside while the rest of the ingredients are prepared. Shell and devein the prawns, leaving the tail fins intact.

Heat a wok, add half the oil, then the peppers and stir-fry for 1–2 minutes, or until crisply tender. Push to one side of the wok. Add the garlic, prawns, chilli (if using) and ginger. Stir-fry until aromatic and prawns are firm, opaque and pink (about 1 minute). Push to the side of the wok. Add the sugar, rice wine, sweet chilli sauce and light soy sauce. Mix the cornflour with 2 tablespoons water, pour it into the wok and heat until glossy and thick (about 1 minute). Stir in the ingredients from the sides of the wok until hot, coated and gleaming. Reduce the heat to very low.

If using the spring onions, finely slice them lengthways and set aside. Drain the noodles thoroughly in a colander. Heat the remaining oil in a wok, add half the spring onions, if using, and the noodles, stir-fry until hot, sizzling and slightly crispy, then add remaining spring onions. Serve the chilli prawns on top of or beside the noodles.

Szechuan, one of the western provinces of China, is famous for its chilli dishes. The sweet, bland taste of squid is balanced beautifully by such spicy treatment. The easy-to-do diamond cross-cuts are a famous feature of Chinese cooking, absorbing the chilli flavour and curling the fish attractively, so don't omit it.

Si Chuan You Yu

Szechuan-style Squid

500 g small to medium squid

1½ teaspoons salt

1 tablespoon egg white, lightly beaten

3 tablespoons cornflour

2 tablespoons peanut oil, plus extra for deep-frying

1 medium-hot red chilli, such as serrano or jalapeño, deseeded and finely sliced

125 ml chicken or fish stock

1 teaspoon sugar

1 teaspoon chilli oil

2 garlic cloves, finely sliced into strips

1 red pepper, deseeded and sliced into long strips or diamonds

2 tablespoons preserved Chinese vegetable, finely sliced

250 g baby broccoli florets or bok choy

Serves 4

To clean the squid, pull the hood away from the tentacles. Pull the 'pen' out of each hood – the pen is a clear almost plastic-like stem, running the length of the hood. Cut off the tentacles just below the eyes, discarding the head and retaining the tentacles.

Slit down the length of the hoods, rinse them well, then open them out. Using a sharp knife, cut slashes diagonally one way, then the other (do not cut all the way through the flesh). Pat the hoods and tentacles dry with kitchen paper.

Mix ½ teaspoon salt, the egg white, 2 tablespoons of the cornflour and 2 tablespoons of the peanut oil in a small bowl and use to rub all over the squid surfaces. Add the chilli.

Mix the stock, sugar, chilli oil and 1 teaspoon salt in a small bowl. Mix the remaining cornflour with 2 tablespoons cold water in a second bowl.

Fill a wok one-third full with peanut oil and heat to 190°C (375°F). Put some of the squid into a frying basket and lower into the hot oil. Cook until curled and set (about 1 minute). Remove and drain on crumpled kitchen paper. Repeat until all the squid are cooked.

Empty all but about 1 tablespoon of the oil out of the wok. Reheat the wok, add the garlic, red pepper, preserved vegetable and broccoli or bok choy and stir-fry for 1 minute. Add the stock mixture and cook for 1 minute more.

Quickly re-mix the cornflour and water, add it to the wok and heat, stirring, until thickened (about 1 minute). Return the cooked squid to the wok, reheat and serve with rice.

Note: Frozen squid, defrosted, are acceptable if no fresh ones are available. Some people remove the pretty purple skin from the squid: I do not, because it looks attractive and tastes good.

Rural China is a land of small farmers and small landholdings. Accordingly, the livestock most easily kept in such conditions is small and free-range. Chickens and pigs, for instance, thrive on kitchen scraps. Ducks might have been specifically designed for use in paddy fields, and in rice-growing areas these waddling flocks, with small boy duck-shepherds in attendance, make a charming and amusing sight.

Pork is the meat most beloved by the majority of Chinese people and features widely on most menus. Formerly, the only beef easily available in China was from water buffalo. In modern

rou lei

poultry and meat

times, juicy, marbled beef has become more readily available, but it remains expensive, and is a special-occasion meat. Mutton and lamb is not widely used in China or South-east Asia, and generally the flavour is not liked in these regions. It is, however, traditionally used by Chinese Muslims (for whom pork is forbidden), Mongols, Manchus and people from Sinkiang.

Meat and poultry are rarely cooked alone, mostly appearing with flavour-and-texture-enhancing vegetables such as bamboo shoots, water chestnuts, onions or mushrooms. Similarly, they are never served alone – rice forms the basis of all meals, and other dishes of meat, poultry and vegetables are served as flavourings or garnishes for rice.

Although the recipe for this famous and deliciously convivial dish is not particularly complex, the organization, preparation and serving need patience and attention. Many people these days prefer, with time at a premium, to buy the pancakes and a ready-glazed, lacquer duck from Chinatown then merely assemble the final whole dish.

Beijing Kao Ya

Peking Duck

2 kg duck, preferably Chinese, patted
   dry with kitchen paper
1 tablespoon dark soft brown sugar
1 teaspoon salt

Pancakes:
250 g plain flour, sifted
250 ml boiling water, allowed to cool
   for 2 minutes
3 tablespoons sesame oil
5–6 tablespoons corn oil, for cooking

Accompaniments:
½ cucumber, cut into 3 cm batons
16 spring onions, white and green
   separate, finely sliced lengthways
150 ml hoisin sauce
1 tablespoon dark soy sauce
1 tablespoon Chinese rice wine or dry
   sherry (optional)
75 ml sweet chilli sauce (optional)
24–30 thin Peking (Chinese-style)
   pancakes, about 250 g

Makes 16, Serves 4–6

If cooking your own duck, hang it up with string or a meat hook through the neck skin or vent and let it dry in a cool, draughty place well away from pets. Leave for 3 hours or overnight. If possible, put it in front of a fan to give an extra blast of cold air for 2 hours longer. Dissolve the sugar and salt in 250 ml hot water, then brush it over the duck, inside and out. Hang the duck to dry for several hours more.

Put a roasting tin in the bottom of the oven and half-fill it with water. Put the duck directly on the rack in the middle of a preheated oven and cook at 200°C (400°F) Gas Mark 6 for 1½ hours, without disturbing or basting. The duck is ready if the juice from the leg, when pierced with a skewer, runs a clear yellow not pink. To carve the duck, first pull off the skin and cut it into serving pieces. Cut the meat off the bones with a cleaver.

If making your own pancakes, put the flour into a large bowl or food processor, then gradually mix in the water until the dough forms a smooth ball. Let stand for 30 minutes, covered, then knead for 3 minutes. Divide the dough into 16 parts and roll into balls. Flatten one with your palm, brush with sesame oil and lightly sandwich another on top. Roll out as a double to 15 cm diameter. Heat a wok or frying pan and brush with the corn oil. Cook the double pancakes for 1–2 minutes per side or until firm and pale. Remove, separate immediately, then stack and keep them warm in a steamer or foil-wrapped in a low oven. Repeat with the remaining dough until all are made. If using ready-made pancakes, brush or spray each one with a little water plus a few drops of sesame oil. Set, folded or flat, in several layers of a steamer and warm through just before serving. If using a ready-prepared duck, wrap it in foil and heat in a moderate oven for 30–40 minutes.

Arrange the meat and skin on a heated serving dish, put the pancakes, cucumber and spring onions on separate dishes, and pour the sauces into small bowls (the hoisin can be served separately, or mixed with the soy sauce and rice wine).

To eat Peking duck, spread a warm pancake with hoisin sauce, add cucumber, spring onion, duck meat and skin, then roll it up and eats it with your fingers.

This is an ancient and time-honoured epicurean way with chicken. Select a really well-flavoured free-range bird (Chinese poultry always tastes marvellous, so try to buy one from Chinatown if you can) and allow time for the marinade to work its flavouring magic. The great advantage of this dish is its convenience – you can cook the dish some hours ahead or even the day before.

Zui Ji

Drunken Chicken

Wipe the chicken with kitchen paper. Remove and discard any trussing strings and the fat near the vent. Put the bird in a colander and pour boiling water into and over the chicken. Drain, then cool in cold water.

To make the stock, put the bird into a large saucepan so it fits snugly. Add the salt, spring onions, ginger, peppercorns, chilli, star anise and 2 litres boiling water. Reheat to boiling point, uncovered, then reduce to a medium simmer, cover and cook for about 40 minutes. Turn off the heat and let cool, without removing the lid.

Lift the bird carefully out of the saucepan and transfer to a large chopping board. Using a Chinese cleaver or heavy knife, cut it carefully in half lengthways, then cut it crossways into 3–5 cm slices. Slide the cleaver under each half, leaving the slices undisturbed, and transfer to a non-reactive shallow dish.

Strain the cooking liquid, measure a quarter into a jug and add all the flavourings except the spring onions. Stir in the rice wine and liquor, then pour over the chicken. Chill at least 1 hour, then serve cold, scattered with pea shoots or finely sliced spring onions.

1 free-range chicken, about 1.5 kg
1 tablespoon sea salt flakes
4 spring onions, quartered
5 cm fresh ginger, unpeeled, finely
    sliced lengthways
1 tablespoon Szechuan peppercorns,
    roasted (page 46)
1 fresh hot red chilli, pierced (optional)
6 whole star anise
4 tablespoons Chinese rice wine
8 tablespoons Gap Liang (Chinese
    sorghum liquor), whisky or brandy
pea shoots or spring onions, to serve

Serves 4

The first time I tasted a dish cooked in this style was when working with Madhur Jaffrey, whose books and television programmes on Far-Eastern and Indian cooking are now legendary around the world. The traditional cooking method for Hunan chicken is stir-frying, but Madhur preferred this deep-frying method instead – the chicken absorbs very little fat but grows beautifully crisp and tender. There is rarely any of this dish left over, it is so delicious!

Hunan Ji

Hunan-style Chicken

Pat the chicken dry with kitchen paper. Pierce each piece 3–4 times through to the bone. Wrap the skin flaps around to make a parcel and secure with cocktail sticks, if preferred.

Mix the ground peppercorns with the sugar, ginger purée, soy sauce and spring onions and rub well into and all over the chicken. Cover and refrigerate for at least 30 minutes, but preferably for 2 hours or even overnight.

Meanwhile, mix all the ingredients for the spicy herbs in a small bowl. To make the soy and sesame sauce, stir the soy sauce, yellow bean sauce, tomato ketchup, stock and vinegar in a second bowl, then add the sugar and sesame oil.

Using a slotted spoon, remove the chicken from the marinade, shaking off any drips. Roll the pieces in the cornflour.

Fill a wok one-third full of oil, heat to 190°C (375°F). Put the chicken pieces, 5 at a time, into a frying basket, and deep-fry in the hot oil for about 16-18 minutes or until dark, crisp and aromatic. Remove from the oil and drain on crumpled kitchen paper. Keep hot in a low oven while you cook the remaining chicken.

To serve, remove the cocktail sticks, pour over the soy and sesame sauce, then sprinkle with the spicy herbs.

Note: In this and many other Chinese dishes, the aromatic Szechuan peppercorns are first toasted in a dry frying pan, or on a baking sheet in the oven. They are then used whole, or ground as in this recipe.

12 chicken thighs, including skin and
    bones, about 1.5 kg
1 tablespoon Szechuan peppercorns,
    dry-toasted (see note opposite),
    then ground
1 teaspoon sugar
2.5 cm fresh root ginger, peeled and
    grated to a pulp
2 tablespoons dark soy sauce
2 spring onions, finely sliced
    crossways
6–8 tablespoons cornflour, to coat
peanut oil, for deep-frying

Spicy Herbs:
2.5 cm fresh root ginger, very finely
    diced
3–4 garlic cloves, finely chopped
3 spring onions, finely sliced
    crossways
3–4 celery stalks with leaves, diced
6 coriander sprigs, chopped
1–2 dried hot chillies, crumbled

Soy and Sesame Sauce:
3 tablespoons light soy sauce
3 tablespoons yellow bean sauce
1 tablespoon tomato ketchup
2 tablespoons chicken stock
2 tablespoons Chinese black vinegar
2 teaspoons sugar
2 teaspoons dark sesame oil

Serves 4–6

This rather grand, special-occasion dish is a Chinese classic – other regional versions are the Steamboat and Chrysanthemum Fire Pot. It takes a little time to assemble, but is fun to serve at a dinner party – feel free to vary the accompaniments and dipping sauces. Each guest should take a piece of meat in their chopsticks and dunk it into the hot stock before dipping in egg yolk, soy sauce and spring onions. The vegetables and bean curd are added gradually to the stock and when all the meat is finished, the soup is ladled into bowls and served separately. Though a spectacular dish, the Fire Pot is relatively easy to assemble.

Huo Guo

Mongolian Fire Pot

1 chilli, fresh or dried, bruised but whole
2.5 cm fresh ginger, sliced lengthways
4 garlic cloves, bruised but whole
2.5 litres boiling lamb or chicken stock
500 g boneless lamb, such as fillet
½ Chinese cabbage, finely sliced
125 g fresh wheat noodles

6–8 spring onions, finely sliced
250 g fresh bean curd, cut in 3 cm dice
4 egg yolks, lightly beaten (optional)
150 ml dark soy sauce
about 250 g bean sprouts

Serves 6

Put a Chinese steamboat on a heatproof tray and set it on the table (making sure the heat cannot damage the surface). Insert red-hot charcoal down the central spout. Heat the chilli, ginger, garlic and stock in a saucepan until boiling, then transfer to the steamboat and cover with the lid. Leave to infuse while the other ingredients are prepared.

Using a cleaver, slice the meat diagonally into paper-thin slices and arrange on a serving platter with the cabbage, noodles, spring onions and beancurd. Put the egg yolk, soy sauce and bean sprouts into separate bowls. When ready to serve, add a handful of spring onions to the stock. Each guest takes a sliver of meat in their chopsticks and places it in the hot stock for 60–90 seconds, then dips it first into the egg yolk, then into the soy sauce and spring onions. When the meat is finished, add the cabbage, bean sprouts, noodles and bean curd to the pot, then serve in soup bowls.

La Jiao Zha Niu Pian

Deep-fried Chilli Beef

Beef has always been a rare and prized ingredient in China, more commonly from water buffalo than from cattle. However, in the West, where it is widely available, this is one of the best-known Chinese beef dishes. The cut used here is a thick, tender steak of rump, fillet or entrecôte, you can experiment with cheaper, less tender but highly flavoured cuts such as flank, blade or skirt. You should cut it thinly and tenderize it in the Chinese way, by marinating it in a mixture of water and baking soda, or in the Western way, with a few teaspoons of vinegar (perhaps rice vinegar, which has a more Chinese flavour). Rub well into the meat before the other flavourings.

To make the beef easier to cut, half-freeze it until firm. Using a Chinese cleaver or other very sharp knife, slice it into wafer-thin strips, across the grain or on the diagonal. Cut these slices crossways into 2 or 3 pieces.

Mix the soy sauce, chilli sauce, chilli, rice wine and cornflour in a bowl. Add the beef strips, toss until well coated, then drizzle over 1 tablespoon of the oil and set aside.

To prepare the vegetables, separate the broccoli into small florets and cut the carrot diagonally into 5 cm thick slices. If using mushrooms, remove and discard the shiitake stems, and cut the larger mushrooms into halves or quarters.

Fill a wok about one-third full of peanut oil and heat to 190°C (375°F), or until a piece of noodle froths up immediately when added to the oil. Add the beef and deep-fry rapidly for 15–30 seconds or until brown outside, part-rare inside. Remove with a slotted spoon and drain on crumpled kitchen paper. Keep the beef warm.

Pour off most of the oil, leaving about 4 tablespoons in the wok. Add the carrots and stir-fry over high heat for 1 minute, then add the broccoli, bamboo shoots and mushrooms, if using, and stir-fry for 1 minute until crisp and tender. Add the sugar, salt and stock or beer, then return the beef to the pan. Reheat briefly, stirring, then serve, sprinkled with sliced spring onions, if using.

300–350 g beef rump steak, fillet
   or entrecôte, cut 1.5 cm thick

1 tablespoon dark soy sauce

2–3 tablespoons hot chilli sauce

1 small fresh hot chilli, deseeded
   and chopped

2 tablespoons Chinese rice wine or
   dry sherry

2 tablespoons cornflour

1 tablespoon chilli oil or peanut oil,
   to help separate the beef slices,

2.5 cm fresh ginger

250 g broccoli

1 medium carrot

175 g fresh shiitake, chestnut or
   large open mushrooms (optional)

250 g canned bamboo shoots,
   drained

1 teaspoon sugar

1 teaspoon sea salt flakes

4 tablespoons beef stock or beer

4 spring onions, finely sliced
   (optional)

peanut oil, for frying

Serves 4

Red-cooking is a classic Chinese cooking technique in which meat or poultry is slowly simmered in a fragrant soy-flavoured stock scented with spices like star anise, cloves, cinnamon and Szechuan peppercorns. A large piece of meat or poultry is first sizzled in hot oil, then simmered in the stock until meltingly tender. The stock can also be frozen and used again and again, becoming more flavourful as time goes on – the stock in some great restaurants has reputedly been used and improved for generations. The meat can also be served cold in its sauce, which usually sets into a delicious jelly.

Qing Jiao Hong Shao Niu Rou

Red-cooked Beef with Peppers

1.5–2 kg beef shin or other boneless braising beef, in one piece

3 tablespoons corn oil

4 garlic cloves, crushed

6 spring onions, halved crossways

5 cm fresh ginger root

1 teaspoon Szechuan peppercorns, roasted (page 46) and ground

6–8 star anise

6–8 cloves, a 5 cm cinnamon stick or a 5 cm strip dried tangerine peel

150 ml beef or chicken stock

240 ml dark soy sauce

60 ml sake or brandy

2 teaspoons sugar

2 teaspoons sea salt flakes

2 peppers, 1 red, 1 yellow, deseeded, and cut in 3 cm dice

Serves 6–8

Pat the beef dry with kitchen paper and tie with string if necessary so it easily fits into the casserole or stockpot.

Heat half of the oil in the casserole or stockpot, add the meat and brown well on all sides. Lift out and remove to a heatproof plate. Add the remaining oil to the pot, then add the garlic, the white sections of the spring onions, the ginger, peppercorns, star anise and the cloves, cinnamon or peel. Stir and cook over a high heat for 2–3 minutes to develop the flavours. Add the stock, soy sauce, sake or brandy, sugar and salt, then boil for about 5 minutes to extract the flavours.

Replace the beef, turn it in the liquid, then return to the boil. Cover with a lid, reduce the heat to low and simmer for 2 hours or until the beef is meltingly tender. Add the pieces of pepper, cover, cook for 30 minutes more, or until very tender and succulent.

Slice the beef and serve with the peppers and a generous spoonful of the cooking liquid. Cut the green parts of the spring onions lengthways, blanch in the cooking liquid if preferred, then add to the beef.

Serve with rice or noodles and a selection of other Chinese dishes.

Chops are the most popular cut of pork in Taiwan, and are often pounded with aromatics such as ginger, garlic, spices and soy, then deep-fried or stir-fried and served on rice or noodles. Another favourite is pork shoulder – sweet, sticky and gelatinous. It is often cooked in a rich stock in the beautiful clay pots known as sand pots, so often seen in Chinese kitchens and on restaurant shelves. If you lack the authentic pot, a large flameproof casserole or stockpot can be used instead. In this stew, a little coconut milk and curry paste offset the sweetness of the meat and the salty flavour of the black beans. Serve with crisp vegetables and plain rice.

Dou Chi Hui Guo Rou

Braised Pork with Black Beans

2 tablespoons peanut or corn oil

2 garlic cloves, chopped

2.5 cm fresh ginger, finely sliced
lengthways

750 g pork shoulder, cut in 3 cm cubes

4 tablespoons brandy or whisky

2 tablespoons dark soy sauce

2 tablespoons Chinese black vinegar

2 teaspoons curry paste

500 ml chicken or beef stock

8 tablespoons canned, unsweetened
coconut milk

2 tablespoons sugar (or rock sugar)

2 tablespoons salted black beans,
crushed

150 g green beans, halved crossways

Serves 4

Heat the oil in a large flameproof casserole or stockpot. Add the garlic and ginger and stir-fry over high heat for 1–2 minutes or until the garlic is golden.

Add the pork, tossing and stir-frying it until well browned all over. Add the brandy or whisky, soy sauce, black vinegar, curry paste and half the stock. Bring to the boil, reduce the heat and simmer, covered, for 40 minutes.

Stir in the coconut milk, sugar, crushed black beans and the remaining stock. Cover with a lid and continue to cook for 25 minutes more. Add the green beans, cover again, cook for a further 5 minutes, then serve.

Also colloquially known as pearl balls or porcupine balls because the raw rice grains stick to the meat, then swell during cooking, so the balls look like a prickly hedgehog or a lion's mane. Water chestnuts and shiitake mushrooms add texture and body to this simple but traditional meat dish. Ideally they should be fresh, but dried mushrooms and canned water chestnuts will do, at a pinch.

Shi Zi Tou

Lion's Head Pork Meatballs

150 g glutinous rice

6 shiitake mushrooms, fresh or dried

8 water chestnuts, fresh or canned

500 g boneless lean pork, minced

1 egg, beaten

1 tablespoon dark soy sauce

½ teaspoon salt

1 teaspoon sugar

1 cm fresh ginger, finely diced

4 spring onions, finely sliced crossways

Serves 4

Put the rice in a bowl, cover with 300 ml cold water, let soak for two hours, then drain.

If using dried mushrooms, put in a small saucepan, cover with boiling water, simmer for 10 minutes or until soft, then drain, discarding the liquid. Remove and discard the mushroom stems, and slice the caps crossways, then into tiny dice.

If using canned water chestnuts, drain them first, then cut into tiny dice. If using fresh water chestnuts peel and discard dark outer skin before dicing the flesh.

Put the mushrooms, water chestnuts, minced pork, egg, soy sauce, salt, sugar, ginger and spring onions in a bowl, then stir and pound until dense. Wet your hands, pinch off balls of mixture about 2.5 cm diameter,then roll the balls in the drained rice, pressing as you roll so they are well covered.

Place a layer of greaseproof paper over the base of a bamboo or metal steamer and arrange the meatballs on top, with about 2 cm space between each one. Cover with tight-fitting lid and put on top of a wok or saucepan filled with boiling water to about 3 cm from the base of the steamer. Steam for 30 minutes, or until the balls are firm and dense and the rice is soft and white. (Add extra boiling water as necessary.)

Serve with several varieties of stir-fried vegetables, including a leafy green such as bok choy, water spinach or spinach.

shu cai

vegetable dishes

Vegetables are often the star attraction in a Chinese meal, and the first accompaniment chosen to complement the almost mystical foundation of rice. They are also cooked in many combinations with meat, fish or poultry, and with each other.

There is a vast range of vegetables available to the Chinese cook, and these ingredients – such as Chinese cabbage, fresh ginger, bean sprouts and bok choy (also known as pak choi), for example – have gradually been incorporated into the Western culinary repertoire. Conversely, it was European traders who first introduced ingredients now intimately associated with Asian cooking, such as chillies, peppers, tomatoes and corn.

China is a huge country with wide variations in climate and terrain, producing an enormous range of vegetables and herbs. Even in city apartment blocks there are tiny plots or window pots of vegetables and fresh herbs. Much emphasis is placed on utter freshness, so vegetables – particularly greens – are gathered as near to the time of cooking as possible, and cooks buy their ingredients every day, or even several times a day.

Interestingly, few vegetables are ever eaten raw and even salads are usually blanched, steamed or stir-fried – perfect methods for preserving colour, flavour and nutrients.

Chinese cooks can draw on a huge range of vegetables. This Cantonese dish uses four kinds of crunchy Oriental greens, and two very different mushrooms – fresh field mushrooms and dried shiitakes. You could also use the romantically named wood ears (also known as cloud ears). Fresh shiitakes could also be used, with a little vegetable stock to take the place of the soaking liquid.

Liang Gu Qing Cai

Chinese Greens with Two Kinds of Mushrooms

25 g dried shiitake mushrooms

¼–½ head Chinese leaves, Chinese cabbage or 1 cos lettuce

250 g Chinese broccoli (gaai lan), flowering cabbage, mustard cabbage (gaai choy), water spinach or other leafy green vegetable

250 g spring greens

125 g mangetout, baby asparagus or sugarsnap peas

2 tablespoons peanut oil

2 teaspoons cornflour

125 g open mushrooms, sliced

2 tablespoons dark soy sauce

1 tablespoon sesame oil

a handful of chives or Chinese garlic chives, chopped (optional)

Serves 4

Put the dried shiitake mushrooms in a bowl, cover with hand-hot water and let soak for about 30–45 minutes until rehydrated, soft and plump. Drain, reserving the soaking liquid. Remove and discard the mushroom stems, cut the caps in half and squeeze dry.

Cut the Chinese leaves, Chinese broccoli and spring greens into 5 cm slices. Cut the mangetout in half diagonally. Wash all greens in cold water and shake dry.

Heat a wok or frying pan, add the oil and heat until just smoking. Add the soaked shiitakes, fresh mushrooms and greens and stir-fry over high heat for 3–4 minutes until hot and just beginning to wilt.

Mix the cornflour with 6 tablespoons mushroom soaking liquid (or water or vegetable stock, if using fresh shiitakes). Stir into the vegetables, together with the soy sauce and sesame oil. Stir-fry for another 30–45 seconds, sprinkle with the chopped chives, and serve with other Chinese dishes.

Stir-frying is a cooking method particularly well suited to green vegetables. It is amazingly quick, and preserves the wonderful colour and crunch, as well as the nutrients like no other. Oyster sauce is a delicious condiment, and canned smoked oysters are a reminder that drying, smoking and pickling are time-honoured Chinese preserving methods, with sharks' fins and birds' nests being just two of the more esoteric dried items.

Hao You Xi Lan Cai

Broccoli in Oyster Sauce

Put the dried shrimp into a mortar and pestle or electric spice-grinder and grind to a powder. Put the cornflour and stock into a small bowl and stir well until dissolved.

Separate the broccoli into small florets, then wash and pat-dry. Heat the oil in a wok or frying-pan, add the broccoli and garlic and stir-fry for about 30–45 seconds.

Add the oyster sauce and the oysters, if using, and cook for a further minute. Stir in the stock and cornflour mixture and, as soon as it thickens, stir in the sesame oil. Sprinkle with the sesame seeds and powdered shrimp, if using, and serve immediately.

1 tablespoon dried shrimp (optional)

2 teaspoons cornflour

2 tablespoons chicken or fish stock

400 g broccoli

3 tablespoons peanut or soy oil

2 garlic cloves, sliced

4 tablespoons oyster sauce

50–75 g shucked fresh oysters, frozen
and thawed, canned and drained or
smoked and drained (optional)

1 teaspoon sesame oil

2 tablespoons toasted sesame seeds

Serves 4

Hua Sheng Chao Bai Cai

Stir-fried Bok Choy with Cashews

A quick, easy vegetable dish which combines complementary qualities –soft and crunchy, bright and dark, salty and sweet, with a pleasant touch of bitterness and slight astringency. Great as a vegetable accompaniment or vegetarian dish. Cashew nuts, native to Central and South America, are just one of the many New World ingredients enthusiastically adopted into the culinary repertoire of cooks all over China, India and South-east Asia.

4 dried shiitake mushrooms, soaked in
   hand-hot water for 20 minutes
3 tablespoons peanut or soy oil
50 g cashew nuts
8–12 baby bok choy, halved lengthways
1 teaspoon salt

1 teaspoon sugar
1 tablespoon dark soy sauce
1 tablespoon oyster sauce
1 tablespoon sesame oil

Serves 4

Drain the shiitakes, reserving some of the soaking liquid. Remove and discard their hard stems, cut the caps in halves or quarters, depending on size, and squeeze them dry.

Heat the oil in a wok or frying pan and stir-fry the cashews, tossing and stirring until dark and crisp. Remove with a slotted spoon and set aside.

Add the bok choy and shiitakes and stir-fry, moving them rapidly around the wok, until crisp and tender. Add the salt, sugar, soy sauce, oyster sauce and sesame oil. Add the cashews, stir in about 2 tablespoons mushroom-soaking water and serve very hot while the nuts are still crisp.

Dou Chi Mo Gu

Mushrooms *with Black Bean Garlic Sauce*

Delicate textures, muted, fascinating colours and
the unusual chewy texture of fried bean curd give this
vegetable dish considerable interest. Do not attempt
this dish using soft bean curd – the correct fried variety
is on sale at Chinese grocers: buy it hard, dry and spongy,
or deep-fry fresh bean curd yourself in advance.

**25 g dried black fungus (cloud
ears, wood ears or tree ears)**

250 g oyster mushrooms, sliced

125 g fried bean curd

1 garlic clove, crushed

2 tablespoons black bean sauce

1 tablespoon hoisin sauce

1 tablespoon light soy sauce

2 teaspoons cornflour

**4–6 tablespoons vegetable or
chicken stock**

3 tablespoons peanut oil

**a small bunch fresh coriander
leaves, torn**

Serves 4

Soak the dried black fungus in hand-hot water for 15–25 minutes or until
rehydrated, soft and large, then drain. Discard the hard central sections and
any gritty parts and cut any large pieces into halves or quarters.

Cut the oyster mushrooms into halves, discarding any tough sections.
Slice the squares of fried bean curd in half then again into halves diagonally.
Mix the garlic, black bean, hoisin and soy sauces together. Mix the cornflour
and stock together in a small bowl. Set aside.

Heat the oil in a wok, add the bean curd, black fungus and mushrooms,
stir-fry briefly, then add the sauces. Heat and gently stir until very hot. Add
the cornflour and stock mixture, and stir gently to form a thickened glaze.
Sprinkle with the torn coriander and serve hot.

Chinese long beans are also known as snake beans, yard-long beans or asparagus beans. They are either pale or dark green, and often as long as your arm. They are sold tied in bundles from the stem end, or tied into coils, but are always cooked in shorter lengths. Long beans have a firm and crunchy texture and are especially good cooked, chilled, and served in salads. If none can be found for this stir-fry dish, then substitute ordinary green beans or even runner beans, cut into 5 cm sections.

Rou Si Dou Jiao

Stir-fried Long Beans *with Dried Shrimp*

500 g long beans or green beans, topped and tailed

3 tablespoons peanut oil

4 garlic cloves, finely sliced

2 fresh hot green chillies, finely sliced crossways

2 pork chops, deboned and sliced crossways into 1 cm strips

25 g dried shrimp (optional)

1 teaspoon salt

1 teaspoon sugar

2 tablespoons light soy sauce

6 tablespoons chicken stock, vegetable stock or water

Serves 4

If using long beans, cut them into 10 cm lengths. If using green beans, leave them whole. Heat the oil in a wok, add the garlic, chillies and pork strips and stir-fry over high heat until the pork is no longer pink. If using dried shrimp, chop them coarsely and add to the wok. Stir in the salt, sugar, soy sauce and stock. Cover the wok and let steam for 2–3 minutes or until the beans are brilliantly green and crunchy. Uncover the pan and stir-fry the beans over moderate heat, until most of the liquid is absorbed or evaporated. Serve hot as an accompaniment.

In China, where the word for rice – *fan* – is synonymous with the word for 'meal', rice cooking has been elevated to a high art, and few meals would be considered balanced without it. Freshly cooked plain white rice has an intrinsic value and taste which is impossible to explain to Westerners. The slightly sticky 'fragrant' rice is preferred by traditional Chinese cooks, and forms a perfect foil for other dishes. However some modern cooks prefer to use long grain rice which cooks into neat, separate grains.

Though most Chinese families eat rice every day, wheat, mung bean or rice flour noodles are also important. Mung bean

mian, fan
noodles and rice

noodles – also known as bean thread, transparent, cellophane, glass or vermicelli noodles – are sold dry in silky, silvery bundles and should be briefly soaked and softened in water before cooking. Rice noodles or rice sticks in many shapes, sizes and thicknesses, both fresh and dried, also need brief soaking in water before cooking. They have a smooth silky texture between the teeth and can give great elegance to a wide range of dishes, since they absorb the surrounding flavours so well. Wheat noodles, often made with egg, are a much more substantial ingredient, and are cooked rather like pasta.

Formerly, noodles were made at home, but today most people buy them ready-made, either dried or fresh, in China and in the West. If using fresh noodles always dip them in boiling water, then drain before using in a recipe.

Dried wheat noodles, made from flour and eggs, have many different names, but are easy to find and are often sold in tightly packed yellow bundles – usually about 8 per 500 g pack. They should be soaked in hot (not boiling) water for 10 minutes to soften evenly, then added to a wok or saucepan of boiling salted water with 1 tablespoon peanut oil to prevent sticking or boiling over. Add the soaked noodles and cook for 3–5 minutes according to the packet instructions or according to their density – thick noodles take longer than thin. Noodles should be bite-tender but firm. If using noodles cold, run them under cold water to stop the cooking process.

Ji Xia Chao Mian

Combination Chow Mein

500 g dried wheat noodles

4 tablespoons peanut oil

6–8 slices rindless smoked
  bacon, chopped

250 g cooked, shelled prawns

4 tablespoons sweet chilli sauce

1 tablespoon hoisin sauce

4 garlic cloves, sliced

2.5 cm fresh ginger, finely sliced
  into batons

2–3 small heads bok choy,
  separated into leaves

4 tablespoons light soy sauce

Serves 4

Soak the noodles, then cook and drain as described above. Heat the oil in a wok, add the bacon and prawns and stir-fry until bacon is crisp and the prawns are hot.

Add the chilli sauce, hoisin sauce, garlic, ginger and bok choy, then stir and toss for about 2 minutes until all the ingredients are hot and crisply tender. Toss in the still-hot, cooked, drained noodles and the soy sauce. Stir-fry and toss until the noodles are well-coated, then serve immediately.

Note: Some instant dried wheat noodles need only one soak-and-cook stage – follow the packet instructions.

Variations:

1. Add scallops and salmon instead of the bacon. Substitute skinned, deseeded red peppers and tomatoes instead of the bok choy, then sprinkle with chives or garlic chives.
2. Use chicken livers and smoked duck or chicken instead of the bacon. Add green peas and a handful of fresh herbs with the bok choy.

Cellophane noodles, made from mung beans, are staples in Northern China. In other areas, these popular noodles, with their slippery, smooth texture, are also called bean threads, glass noodles, silver noodles or transparent noodles. Some are hair-thin, some like slim ribbons, some wide strips, others flat sheets. They soak up other flavours beautifully.

Jiang Wo Ju Fen Si

Cellophane Noodles with Lettuce and Ginger

Put the noodles in a bowl, cover with hot water and soak for 10–15 minutes. Alternatively, soak for 20 minutes in cold water, then drain and scissor-cut in half.

Heat half the oil in a wok, stir-fry the garlic and ginger for 1 minute until golden, then add the sesame paste, soy sauce and sesame oil. Stir in the hot stock. Add the noodles and cook for 1–2 minutes.

Meanwhile heat the remaining oil in a second wok or frying pan, add the radicchio, lettuce, daikon, spinach, chilli and pepper. Stir-fry quickly, then toss into the noodles, mix well and serve.

50 g (about 2 bundles) cellophane noodles
2 tablespoons corn oil
2 garlic cloves, finely sliced
5 cm fresh ginger, finely sliced
2 tablespoons Chinese sesame paste
2 tablespoons dark soy sauce
2 teaspoons sesame oil
90 ml hot chicken stock
1 head radicchio or red lettuce, sliced
1 cos lettuce, finely sliced
75 g daikon (mooli), cut into 5 cm batons
6 spinach leaves, finely sliced
1 green medium-hot chilli, such as serrano
freshly ground black pepper

Serves 4

Ya Pu Liang Ban Mian

Vermicelli Noodle Salad *with Duck Breast*

Usually, rice noodles are softened slowly in cold water then heated or cooked in boiling water just before serving. This recipe can be done much more quickly – the noodles are soaked for a shorter time in hot water then cooked very briefly with the remaining aromatics. For an easy, excellent dish, use smoked duck breast, or pan-fry or char-grill fresh duck. Other ingredients could also be used – try cooked chicken, or stir-fried pork strips, squid or prawns.

250 g thin rice stick vermicelli noodles

3 tablespoons corn oil

4 shallots, chopped

2.5 cm fresh ginger, finely sliced
   lengthways

8–12 fresh shiitake mushrooms, stems
   discarded, caps sliced

350 g smoked duck breast, sliced

1 small head spring cabbage, bok choy
   or Chinese leaves, finely sliced

4 spring onions, sliced lengthways

1 tablespoon light soy sauce

250 ml chicken stock

1 teaspoon sugar

1 teaspoon salt

1 tablespoon chopped fresh parsley

1 tablespoon chopped fresh chives or
   Chinese chives

1 tablespoon chopped fresh coriander
   leaves

Serves 4

Put the noodles in a bowl, cover with hot water for 6–8 minutes (any longer and they will soften too much). Drain just before using, and while they are still warm scissor-cut them into half lengths to make handling easier.

Working quickly, heat the oil in a wok, add the shallots and ginger, stir-fry briskly for 2 minutes, then add the mushrooms and smoked duck. Cook, covered, for 1 minute.

Add the cabbage, spring onions and warm noodles. Add the soy sauce, chicken stock, sugar and salt. Cook until the liquid is absorbed – about 2–3 minutes. Serve hot, warm or cold, sprinkled with the herbs.

Hokkien Mee are the mad, chaotic tangle of thick yellow wheat flour noodles, sold dried in Asian grocers and larger supermarkets. They are always par-boiled, drained and dried, before use. They are good in soups, as an accompaniment, or in fried noodle dishes, such as chow mein. The tangy Chinese dried sausage (lap cheong), though it looks like a mini-salami, must be cooked before use.

Ke Jia Chao Mian

Hokkien Stir-fried Noodles

500 g fresh wheat noodles, such as Hokkien Mee

1 pair Chinese sausages (lap cheong)

5 tablespoons peanut oil

4 garlic cloves, thinly sliced

250 g fresh bean sprouts

4 tablespoons dark soy sauce

3 tablespoons Chinese white vinegar

3 tablespoons chicken stock or water

2 fresh red chillies, deseeded and finely sliced lengthways

2 eggs, lightly beaten

2 tablespoons chopped fresh Chinese garlic chives

4 tablespoons torn fresh coriander leaves

Serves 4

Heat the noodles in a saucepan of boiling water for 2 minutes. Drain in a colander, then tip out onto a flat surface to dry. When dry, break them into clumps.

Meanwhile steam or briefly boil the Chinese sausages for 5 minutes, drain and cut into thin diagonal slices.

Heat 4 tablespoons of the oil in a wok and swirl to coat well. Add the garlic and bean sprouts and stir-fry until aromatic and wilted, add the sausage slices and stir-fry until lightly coloured and aromatic. Add the clumps of noodles. Stir-fry until they change colour – about 1 minute.

Mix the soy sauce, vinegar, stock and chillies in a small bowl, then pour over the noodles, tossing and stirring. Transfer the noodles to serving plates and keep hot.

Quickly rinse and dry the wok, return it to the heat, and add the remaining oil. Pour the beaten eggs into the hot wok and stir them quickly over the heat until just set. Cut into thin slices. Sprinkle the egg strips, chives and coriander over the noodles and serve hot.

The Chinese use leftover rice in a variety of ways – fried rice is a favourite, but one which excites huge controversy and discussion. The secret is to use recently cooked rice, which is cool, rather than hot or cold, and it shouldn't be too damp or too dry either. Cooked this way, it can be in a class all by itself. This version is colourful, delicious and easy, and you can vary the components according to what's fresh and in season. Serve soy and chilli sauces separately.

Chao Fan

Chinese Fried Rice

4 tablespoons corn oil

1 egg, beaten

1 onion, finely sliced

2 spring onions, finely sliced

2 garlic cloves, finely sliced

2.5 cm fresh ginger, finely sliced
(optional)

2 cups recently cooked white rice, about
425–450 g

125 g cooked asparagus or green beans,
sliced into 3 cm pieces

125 g corn niblets (optional)

2 ripe red tomatoes, skinned, deseeded
and diced

350 g cooked chicken, shelled prawns or
crabmeat, or a mixture of all three

To serve:

soy sauce

sweet chilli sauce

Serves 4

Put 2 tablespoons of the oil into a hot wok and heat well. Add the beaten egg and stir constantly over the heat. Using a slotted spoon, lift out and remove the cooked, browned egg, slice finely, and set aside while the other ingredients are prepared.

Heat the remaining oil in the wok. Add the onion, spring onions, garlic, ginger, if using, and the cooked rice. Stir-fry over high heat for 2 minutes.

Add the asparagus or beans, corn, if using, and tomatoes. Add 125 ml water, then the chicken, prawns or crabmeat, and the cooked egg. Cover the wok with a lid, reheat for about 1–2 minutes, then serve hot with little dishes of soy sauce and sweet chilli sauce, served separately.

tian dian xin

puddings

Though the Chinese have a fierce sweet tooth, and adore cakes and puddings and other sugary dishes, they do not serve these foods at the end of a meal as Westerners do.

Most sweet puddings make their appearance at formal banquets and are served, not at the end, but part-way through, in between the savoury dishes. Even custard tarts appear with other dim sum dishes as part of yum cha, the traditional family restaurant outing of breakfast-combined-with-lunch.

The usual finish to a family meal – and even some in restaurants – is a simple plate of fresh fruit, such as wedges of orange. Scented, smooth and silky-textured fruits are prized in China, and these are also popular, simply prepared, sliced or with ginger syrup or fruit juice. Lychees, rambutans, mangosteens, longans, rose apples, starfruit, custard apples, persimmons, mangoes, guavas, Asian pears, apples, loquats, kumquats, pomelos and other citrus fruits, as well other delicacies are now easily available from Asian markets or specialist fruiterers.

The dishes given here would not usually be served at the end of a traditional Chinese meal, but are delicious treats for Westerners used to finishing a meal with sweet dishes. Nothing could be more typically Chinese than toffee fruits – in this case apples – while almond junket, often served in neat cubes in China, is served here as a pudding with typical Chinese fruits.

Many people end a celebration meal at a Chinese restaurant with this simple but superb treat. It is worth learning to do it well, so choose flavourful, crisp apples. You can arrange this dish so everyone cooks their own at the table – have all the ingredients prepared and on the table, together with bowls of iced water to set the toffee. Alternatively, for a more sober presentation, prepare the dish ahead and take it to the table complete, as here.

Tang Pingguo

Toffee Apples

4 sweet apples, such as Cox's, Gala or Braeburn

6 tablespoons plain flour

1 tablespoon cornflour or rice flour

2 egg whites, beaten to a froth

125 g caster sugar

2 tablespoons water

1 tablespoon lard

2 tablespoons white sesame seeds or black sesame seeds

peanut or corn oil, for deep-frying

a bowl of iced water, for setting toffee

Serves 4

Peel and core the apples and cut each one into 4, 6 or 8 pieces depending on size. Roll in 2 tablespoons of the flour to coat well.

Whisk the remaining flour with the cornflour and egg whites to form a light batter.

Fill a wok one-third full of oil and heat to 190°C (375°F) or until a piece of noodle puffs up immediately. Dip each piece of apple into the batter and lower carefully into the hot oil. Deep-fry in batches for 3 minutes each, then remove and drain on kitchen paper.

Put the sugar and water into a small saucepan and heat until dissolved. Add the lard. Increase the heat to high and cook, stirring with chopsticks occasionally, until a golden-red coloured toffee or caramel forms. Turn off the heat.

Dip each piece of deep-fried apple into the caramel (as it darkens and thickens, it will cling better to the battered surface), then sprinkle each piece with sesame seeds. Dip briefly in iced water to set the toffee, then serve.

Although European junket is usually set with rennet, this pale and delicate Chinese junket is set with gelatin. Lychees and persimmons are native to China, though the word persimmon comes from the North American Algonquin language. Wait until persimmons are very ripe, or they taste bitter and furry, though there are some modern varieties without this characteristic. The bright orange, beautifully named persimmon is also known less attractively as as kaki fruit or sharon fruit.

Xing Ren Dou Fu

Almond Junket with Persimmons and Lychees

Dissolve the gelatin in 6 tablespoons of cold water and leave to swell and set. Heat, with half of the evaporated milk or coconut milk in a saucepan, stirring, over moderate heat. Alternatively, put in a non-metal bowl or jug and microwave on HIGH for 60–75 seconds using an 800 watt machine.

Add the remaining evaporated milk or coconut milk, sugar and almond essence and stir well. Pour into 4 serving dishes and chill in the refrigerator until set.

To serve, remove the dishes from the refrigerator and pile the fruit on top.

1 sachet gelatin granules (12 g)
300 ml evaporated milk or canned
   coconut milk
50 g caster sugar
1 teaspoon almond essence
1 or 2 ripe fresh persimmons, diced,
   or 450 g canned, drained and diced
16 ripe fresh lychees, deseeded,
   or 450 g canned and drained

Serves 4

Index